4

William Albright

Sweet Sixteenths
A Concert Rag for Organ

EXCLUSIVELY DISTRIBUTED BY

7777 W. BLUEMOUND RD. P.O. BOX 13819 MILWAUKEE, WI 53213

SWEET SIXTEENTHS
(A Concert Rag for Organ)

WILLIAM ALBRIGHT

Sw: Flutes and Strings 8' (p)
Gt: Flute, Principal 8'(mp)
Pos: 8', $2\frac{2}{3}$' (mf)
Ped: Flutes 16', 8'
Swell to Pedal, Great, and Positiv

6

(1975)

8-84088-60110-2

U.S. $7.99

ISBN 978-1-4584-1384-0

50799

HL00220361